W9-DHS-990

– THE –
LITTLE RED
RIDING HOOD
REBUS BOOK

retold by Ann Morris

pictures by

Ljiljana Rylands

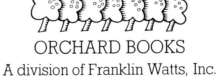

ORCHARD BOOKS
A division of Franklin Watts, Inc.
New York & London

Text copyright © 1987 by Ann Morris
Illustrations copyright © 1987 by Ljiljana Rylands
First American edition 1987
All rights reserved. No part of this book may be reproduced or
transmitted in any form or by any means, electronic or mechanical,
including photocopying, recording or by any information storage or
retrieval system, without permission in writing from the Publisher.

ORCHARD BOOKS
387 Park Avenue South
New York, New York 10016

Orchard Books Canada
20 Torbay Road
Markham, Ontario 23P 1G6

Orchard Books is a division of Franklin Watts, Inc.

Book design by Jennifer Campbell

The text of this book is set in 18pt Rockwell Light.
The illustrations are black line colored pencil.

10   9   8   7   6   5   4   3   2   1

Library of Congress Cataloging-in-Publication Data

Morris, Ann, 1930 –
  Little Red Riding Hood.

  Based on the original story: Rotkäppechen.
  Summary: A rebus version of the fairy tale about the
little girl who meets a hungry wolf in the forest, in
which pictures are substituted for some words or parts
of words.
  [1. Fairy tales.   2. Folklore – Germany.   3 Rebuses
I. Rylands, Ljiljana, ill.   II. Rotkäppchen.   III. Titl
PZ8.M8287Li 1987   398.2'1 [E]   87 - 7696
ISBN 0-531-05730-5
ISBN 0-531-08330-6 (lib. bdg.)

Printed in Belgium

How to read

THE LITTLE RED RIDING HOOD REBUS BOOK.

This story is a wonderful puzzle to solve! Words or parts of words are replaced by very small pictures, letters or numbers. Basket becomes 🧺, because 🐝cause, you U, ate 8 and so on.

If you can't work out the meaning of a word, just look it up in the rebus dictionary at the end. Here you will find a list of all the rebus words in the story in the order in which they first appear.

Then, if you look carefully, you can have fun picking out the tiny objects which are shown again in the big pictures.

Now read and Njoy *The* 🧥 *Rebus* 📘!

Once upon a time there was a **1**derful little girl called . She lived with her  in the country in a small  with a  filled with .

Do U know Y she was called ? It was cause her who loved her very much, had made her a warm cape with a hood that covered her head. wore it everywhere.

Her lived in the next at the other Nd of the . liked 2 visit 's and 2 play with her roly-poly .

1 morning her said, " has a very bad cold. want U 2 take her this of home-made and a of m best jam. Now, run along, but don't er off the 2 play or 2 pick the . U have a long way 2 go."

's  gave her a kiss. Then she set off with her  of  and  jam over her arm and her  cape wrapped around her.

The  was shining through the 🌳🌳, lighting the 🌲🌲 🐝4 her. She could hear 🐦🐦 singing, cheep! cheep! and the 🪓🛢️ working nearby, choppity chop! choppity chop! Bright 🌼🌻🌷 were growing everywhere. She wanted 2 stop and pick them but her 👧 had told her not 2 ⭐/er off the 🌲🌲.

She had not gone far in **2** the 🌲 when she met a 🐺 who seemed friendly. "Good morning, 🐺," said 🧕. "Isn't it a beautiful day!"

But the 🦊 was not really friendly. He was sneaky and mean and very hungry! If it hadn't been **4** the sounds of the 🪓🪓 he would have **E10** 🧒 then and there. But instead he called out, "Good morning, little girl. Where **R** **U** going?"

"👁'm taking this home-made 🍞 and 🍓 jam **2** m👁👵 in the 🏘 at the **N**d of the 🌲🌲🌲," said 🧒.

The hungry 🐺 looked at 🧒. He grew even more hungry when he 🪚 the 🧺 of home-made 🍞 and the 🫙 of 🍓 jam. He licked his lips and long whiskers as he thought about such tasty morsels. "👁'll have the little girl and her 👵 4 m👁 dinner," he said 2 himself greedily.

The hungry  ran straight **2** 🧓's 🏠 and

knocked on the 🚪, knock! knock!

"Who's there?" said 👩.

"It is 🧒," said the 🐺 in a squeaky voice,

trying **2** sound like a little girl. "👁 have brought

U a 🧺 of good things **2 E**t."

"Just lift the latch and come in," said  whose cold was 2 bad 4 her 2 notice how strange the voice sounded.

The hungry rushed in 2 's room and 8 her up in 1 big gulp. He put on 's and her and jumped in 2 2 wait 4 the next part of his meal. And U know what that was, don't U? It was !

By now 🧥 was halfway through the 🌲.

She felt so happy walking in the warm ☀shine,

listening 2 the 🐦🐦 singing, and waving 2 her

animal friends that she 4 got her 👧 had told her

not 2 go off the 🌳 2 play or pick 🌺.

"👁'll just stop and pick a few for 👵," 🧥 said

2 herself. "They will cheer her up." And she

picked a large bunch of 🌼, 4 get-me-nots

and all the 🌺 that 👵 loved best. She placed

them carefully on the top of the 🧺 with the

home-made 🍞 and the 🫙 of 🍓 jam. Then she

walked on 2 👵's.

When  finally reached 's  she knocked on the . Knock! Knock!

"Who's there?" said a gruff voice that didn't sound very much like .

When she heard the gruff voice she thought  must have a very bad cold. "It's me, ," she said.

"Just lift the latch and come in, m ," said the strange voice.

So  lifted the latch and went in2 the dark room.

She couldn't ,  the  were drawn
and she had a  pulled down over her face.

"How are ? 've brought some of

's home-made and a of her best

jam. They will make strong again," said .

"Come and sit near me," said the .

put the of good things on a and sat

down next  the . By now she knew that

something was not quite right.

"Oh , what big M U have," she said.

"All the better 2 hear U with, m👁 child."

"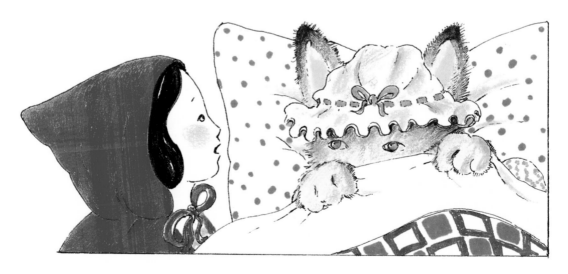, what big 👁👁 U have."

"All the better 2 C U with, m👁 child."

"And , what big U have!"

"All the better 2 E t U with!" said the .

And he sprang out of and gobbled up .

Then he fell fast asleep and snored so loudly

could almost hear him in the next .

Some time later  of the 🪓🏺 came  👵's 🏠. He had heard the loud noise as he worked nearby and 1dered if anything was the matter.

He went inside and what do U th he ?

It was the —still asleep and snoring loudly.

"'ll take care of U," said the . And he slit

open the 's belly with his large hunting

Out jumped a little girl in a  cape.

"Oh, it's U 🧍," said the 🪓.

"It was so dark in there and 👁 was frightened,"

she said. "Look, 🧕 is in there **2**." The 🪓 quickly

pulled her out.

 was very tired but she was glad 2

back in her own home with her  grandchild

by her side.

Last of all, the  took some large

and filled the 's belly with them, and sewed

up the place where he had cut him open. The

, who would never  hungry again, died.

Then , and the the home-made and the jam. 's cold got better. And knew she must never er off the again.

REBUS DICTIONARY

The rebuses in this dictionary are in the order

they first appear in the story.

wonderful **1**derful   red

 Little Red Riding Hood   village

mother   end **N**d

house   wood

garden   to, too **2**

flowers   cottage

you **U**   cat

why **Y**   one **1**

because cause   I

grandmother   basket

bread

jar

my m[eye]

strawberry

wander [wand]er

path

sun

trees

before [bee]4

birds

wood-cutters

into in2

wolf

for 4

eaten E10

are R

I'm [eye]'m

saw

I'll [eye]'ll

door

eat E t

ate 8

nightie

night cap

bed

forgot	**4**got	ears	
daisies		eyes	
forget-me-nots		teeth	
4get-me-nots		wondered	**1**dered
dear		think	th
see	C	wood-cutter	
curtains		knife	
I've	've	be	
table		stones